FREESIAS

By

W. F. McKENZIE

FREESIAS

New hybrid freesias

Contents

ACKNOWLEDGEMENTS   9

1. HISTORY AND DEVELOPMENT OF THE
   FREESIA   11

2. ECONOMIĊ CONSIDERATIONS   17

3. SYSTEMS OF PRODUCTION   22

4. RAISING FREESIAS FROM SEED   29

5. RAISING FREESIAS FROM CORMS   36

6. GENERAL MANAGEMENT   40

7. PESTS AND DISEASES AND OTHER
   TROUBLES   43

8. FREESIA GROWING FOR AMATEURS   48

INDEX   53

Illustrations

NEW HYBRID FREESIAS   *frontispiece*

1. A FINE SPRAY   *facing page* 12
2. FREESIAS FOR HOME DISPLAY   13
3. GROWING FROM CORMS, GENERAL LAYOUT   28
4. METHOD OF SUPPORTING FREESIAS   29
5. PICKING THE BLOOMS   32
6. GROWN FROM SEED   33
7. PREPARING FOR PACKING IN CORNWALL   40
8. PACKING FOR MARKET IN CORNWALL   41
9. ANOTHER FORM OF PACKING, CORRUGATED FIBREBOARD   44
10. PRIZE WINNER IN GUERNSEY, BEST EXHIBIT IN SHOW   45

1. *History and Development of the Freesia*

THE FREESIA does not have a very long history, and probably it was first recorded in print by the Austrian botanist, Jaquin, in his book, *Scones Plantarum Rariorum*, which was published in 1790. It was illustrated under the name of *Gladiolus refractus*. An English botanist placed it in the genera *Tritonia*, and another botanist in the genera *Ixia*. It seems that no one knew quite where to place it apart from the fact that it was obviously in the natural order *Iridaceae*.

It was a German botanist, Klatt, who in 1866 finally decided it was a new genera and called it Freesia after the horticulturally-minded German physician Friedrich Henriech Theodor Freese of Keil.

Freesia *Refracta* was grown for its very sweet scent rather than for its other attributes. In colour, F. *Refracta* is soft creamy yellow and it is not a very prepossessing flower.

Other freesias known at this period included F. *Aurea*, F. *Leichtlinii*, and F. *Armstrongii*. F. *Armstrongii* was found in South Africa in 1897, and was named after its finder, a Mr. Armstrong. It had small red flowers of no great beauty, but it was to prove of great importance to the hybridist because of its colour.

It was brought to Kew Gardens and crossed with F. *Leichtlinii*, and though this cross gave rise to new coloured freesias, these hybrids did not raise any real enthusiasm.

Dr. Ragioneri of Florence had taken up freesia breeding in Italy and had achieved success with a hybrid which was the result of crossing F. *Leichtlinii* with F. *Refracta var alba*. Dr. Ragioneri gave hybrids to a French market gardener who developed them very successfully.

In Holland, C. Van Tubergen of Haarlem, began breeding freesias in 1901 and produced a very fine strain which is still popular.

There have been other pioneers in freesia breeding and among them we must not forget two Englishmen, Mr. G. H. Dalrymple of Southampton, and Mr. F. N. Chapman.

Among the fine strains available today, we must note the following:

> Konynenburg & Mark (K. & M. strain)
> Parigo Horticultural Co., Spalding (Parigo strain)
> Alois Frey, California (Rainbow strain)
> Ragioneri, Florence (Ragioneri strain)
> Messrs. Tubergen, Holland (Tubergen's strain)

There are a very large number of named varieties available today, but these must be grown from corms as they do not come true from seed. They are very good for breeding purposes, and improving strains of seed. The following is a fairly comprehensive list of modern varieties in alphabetical order:

Afterglow	Orange red
Albatre	White with long stems
Alison Johnson	White
Amethyst	Lavender
Apogee	Primrose
Apotheose	Lilac mauve
Beauty	Soft mauve pink
Blushing Bride	Creamy white
Buttercup	Primrose yellow and orange
Caro Carlee	Cream

Plate 1.   A fine spray

Plate 2. Freesias for home display

Celesti	Pale blue and lilac
Charmantè	Apricot
Côte d'Azur	Blue with long stems
Destiny	Primrose
Eldred's Giant White	Large white flowers, well scented
Goldcup	Yellow, good scent
Golden Fleece	Yellow and orange, well scented
Golden Sovereign	Deep golden yellow
Gwendolyn	Pink
Helios	Deep yellow
Ivory Gem	Ivory
Insulinde	Deep orange
Jewel	Magenta
King Cup	Orange yellow
La Froppante	Lavender with white throat
Lady Carew Pole	Salmon pink
Laura E. Richardson	Pale blue
Magnificance	Mauve
Maryon	Soft blue
Maureen	Heliotrope
Mouelle	Violet rose
Neptune	White, tall grower
Old Rose	Pink
Orange Nassau	Yellow and orange
Orange Princess	Yellow, edged orange scarlet
Orange Sun	Tawny orange, long stems
Prince of Orange	Yellow orange, blotched
Princess Marizke	Orange, with long stems
Princess Marie Jose	Salmon and orange

B

Red Riding Hood	Dark red
Robinetta	Violet red
Rosabella	Red rose
Rosalind	Pink, dwarf grower
Souvenir	Primrose yellow
The Bride	White
Tubergeni	Carmine rose
Violetta	Purple violet
Wistaria	Violet blue
Yellow Hammer	Yellow, good scent, with long stems

Some maintain that intensive breeding is destroying the scent of the freesia, perhaps its most valuable trait, for we must agree that, however lovely the colours are, a bunch of 12–15 stems of freesias do not have the appeal of 12–15 carnations or roses. Continuous breeding has largely lost the scent in roses and the same may be happening to freesias. The red and blue shades do not have much scent, and one must go to the yellow and orange varieties for this attribute. The old F. *Refracta* was grown for its scent, and was a feature of large private gardens where it was extensively grown. Thus scent was the real reason for its cultivation because the flower itself possessed no great beauty and its colour was rather insipid. This shows that scent appeals greatly to a number of people.

We must agree that the lovely colours now available make up to a certain extent for the loss of scent.

The freesia, of course, is still being developed, and will go on improving for many decades to come. There are some very fine named varieties in the yellow and orange hues, but the reds and blues can be considerably improved in size, hue, and scent production. Named varieties can be propagated from corms only as they do not usually come true from seed. They are too expensive for cut-flower production. Seeds do come fairly true to colour and specialists offer separate colours.

Some varieties are very susceptible to virus disease and have to be destroyed. Virus is believed not to be carried in the seed, but new varieties can become infected through contact with diseased plants, particularly if aphis is present.

The cultivation of freesias for cut flowers has increased tremendously since the late war, and is developing each year. Concurrently with this increase in production, there is an increase in public demand, which is fortunate, for otherwise the market would be over supplied, and prices would fall below the cost of production. In Denmark, production increased ten times during the ten years from 1940 to 1950. No one can say when saturation point will be reached in Britain but it should not happen yet, though production and demand are rather close.

How much people will pay for freesias is an important question? At the present time, they are paying quite high prices in the larger florists, and the author has noted occasional grumbles from retail customers. The difference between the wholesale and retail price increases or decreases with the type of florist and the locality.

Freesias have a very long season of flowering, and some growers produce flowers from seed as early as August, while other growers are still cutting flowers in April, generally from corms planted in September. It is difficult to say whether a short or long season favours a particular flower. We have carnations all the year round, but carnations are still among the most popular flowers on the home market.

In Great Britain there are certain periods when people buy flowers in quantity. These are around Armistice Day, Christmas, Mothering Sunday (late March) and Easter. The reasons are obvious as these are the times when people celebrate or commemorate and also because there are large numbers of weddings at Christmas and Easter. At other periods many of the ordinary public seem to ignore flowers. We must remember that flowers are luxuries to very many people and are expensive during the winter period. Freesias are expensive and with efficient production methods growers could probably manage on lower prices for their flowers, and retailers could manage on lower profit margins if they had a larger number of sales.

2. *Economic Considerations*

ANY GROWER who may be considering growing freesias is most interested in the economics of the crop, and also how it will affect his present cropping system and his crop rotations. Without some fundamental knowledge of costs and returns, he cannot decide whether it would pay him or suit his methods to cultivate freesias.

The following are among the most important questions to a potential grower.

a) Will his glasshouses be suitable for freesias?
b) How will they affect his labour force?
c) Will they pay better than one of the crops he is now growing?
d) What will the capital outlay be?
e) Will they compete with or affect his other crops?

Most glasshouses are suitable for freesia growing as they are modest in their demands. If a temperature of 50° F. can be maintained in severe weather, that will be enough. They should be in fair condition and capable of allowing plenty of light to enter the houses in the winter months.

Whether freesias would affect his labour can only be answered by the grower himself. If he grows from seed, labour will be needed in April or May for pre-chitting and sowing the seed, also for watering during the summer. Women labour will probably be used for fixing supports, cutting flowers and packing. This will occur during the winter months, generally from October to February.

If corm production is contemplated, there will be no labour requirement until the end of August when the corms must be planted. Little further labour will be necessary until the plants are ready for stringing. Most of the work will be done when the first flowers are ready to market.

Women labour is used by most growers not only because their cost is about two-thirds only of male labour—women are more nimble fingered than men and are quick and effective for picking and bunching the flowers. Freesia should never be roughly handled for they are rather fragile flowers. Growers find that the growing of freesias provides useful and profitable employment for their women workers when otherwise they would be almost idle. In these days of labour shortage, no grower likes to lose his best workers because he has no work and cannot afford to keep them on.

On a large nursery it is useful to put one of the foremen in charge of the freesias, and allocate him the necessary labour when required. On smaller nurseries the owner himself will supervise their cultivation. The foreman selected should be interested in flowers, and it is desirable that he should be interested in freesias. He should have had training in the craftsmanship of horticulture and have done considerable propagation work with other crops. It is doubtful if a man who has never had any basic horticultural training will make a good freesia grower.

Many nursery owners are not suited to specialised flower crops like the freesia. Their methods may be slapdash and the importance of correct timing of operations may mean nothing to them. Growers of this type should leave freesias alone.

Whether freesias will pay better than one of the grower's present crops is difficult to answer. It depends on how well he grows his present crop and how long it will take him to learn how to grow freesias really well. It might be best to grow a pilot crop first and see how well it could be produced on his nursery, before changing from a crop which he knows is fairly profitable. It is acknowledged in horticulture that every year is different—different in its weather and in its prices for crops grown. A gross return of £7,000 to £8,000 per acre would be fair at the present time. In a few years it may be much lower! The old law of supply and demand can never be ignored or disregarded. It is true to say that the freesia is becoming more popular with the public but it is still expensive judged against other flowers.

The capital outlay for freesias is considerable, and for seed would be very much less than for corms. For corms, the cost would be approximately £2,500 per acre. The other expenses would be in the region of those for other flower crops. Of course, the cost of seed and corms would be spread over several years as the same stock would be grown for five years or more in normal circumstances.

How freesia growing will affect other crops in the nursery depends on the other crops. Freesias can be fitted into various rotations, and are grown as 'second' crops, but as it will be May or even June before plants grown in the soil can be lifted for storage, they will affect following crops. Freesias can follow on early crops of tomatoes, or normal crops of cucumbers, gladioli, or other spring flowers under glass. But it is in the following spring that difficulties may arise if the houses are not ready until the end of May or early June. It will then be too late for tomatoes, but a second crop of cucumbers can be planted. Late struck chrysanthemums can be grown and these may be planted from the end of June until the beginning of August.

If freesias are grown in pots (see chapter on Systems of Production) and planted in the houses in early September, they can follow tomatoes, cucumbers, or any other crop which is being pulled out then. Freesias can be grown in carnation beds, so they could follow that crop. Freesias grown in boxes can be lifted into houses in September and when they have finished flowering the boxes can be removed to an outdoor position so that the foliage may die down naturally.

Plenty of water must be given to keep the plants going until the new corms are fully formed. Of course, the corms will not be so well grown as those which have been produced on plants allowed to remain *en situ* until ripened.

Where mobile houses are available, there will be little difficulty about rotations. Freesias could be fitted into rotation systems as suggested below ·

Freesias	September–April	1st year
Tomatoes	April–September	2nd year
Chrysanthemums	September–December	2nd year
Lettuce	January–April	3rd year
Tomatoes	April–September	3rd year
Freesias	September–April	3rd year

Freesias are fairly prolific and can give about three flower stems for every two plants. Some growers cut the large sideshoots and market these at lower prices per bunch, and in these cases the number of shoots per plant would be much higher. The returns from bunches of freesias over a whole cropping season may vary very greatly, for so much depends on quality. The study of prices from the weekly horticultural journals shows that prices per bunch can vary from 1/– to 6/–. A grower who produces high quality freesias can sell his crop for prices from 2/6 to 6/–.

WHOLESALE PRICES PER BUNCH OF 12 SPIKES
(*taken from* 'The Commercial Grower' *reports*)

SEASON 1955–1956

| 9 September | 2/6 – 4/– | 6 January | 3/6 – 5/– |
| 16 | 4/– – 5/– | 13 | 2/6 – 4/6 |

23		4/- - 5/-	20	2/- - 4/6
30		3/6 - 4/-	27	1/6 - 4/-
7	October	4/- - 4/6	3 February	2/- - 3/-
14		4/- - 5/-	10	1/6 - 3/-
21		6/- - 7/-	17	1/6 - 3/-
28		6/- - 8/-	24	2/6 - 3/6
4	November	5/- - 6/-	2 March	2/- - 3/6
11		4/- - 5/-	9	2/- - 3/6
18		3/6 - 5/-	16	2/- - 3/-
25		4/6 - 6/-	23	1/6 - 3/6
2	December	4/6 - 6/-	30	1/- - 3/6
9		3/- - 5/-	6 April	2/- - 3/6
16		3/6 - 5/-	13	1/- - 2/6
23		4/- - 6/-	20	1/- - 2/6
			27	1/- - 2/6

1956–1957 SEASON

7 September	4/- - 6/-	9 November	2/- - 4/6
14	2/- - 6/-	16	2/6 - 5/-
21	2/6 - 5/-	23	2/6 - 5/-
28	2/- - 5/-	30	1/6 - 4/6
5 October	2/- - 5/-	7 December	1/6 - 4/-
12	3/- - 5/-	14	1/6 - 3/6
19	2/6 - 5/-	21	1/6 - 5/-
26	2/- - 4/-	28	2/6 - 5/-
2 November	2/- - 4/6		

3. *Systems of Production*

THERE ARE a number of ways of producing freesias but all commercial methods entail marketing flowers from August or September to April. The earliest flowers are from April-sown plants, while corms do not usually produce flowers before February and may give flowers until the end of April if planted fairly late. We can divide freesia growing into production from seed and production from corms.

The advantages of seed-produced plants include earlier flowering and cheapness, while the disadvantages are greater time in producing any returns, and seeds do not come true as corms will do; and in the hands of an unskilled grower, losses during germination can be heavy. Cases are known here of very poor germination—as low as 10 per cent or even less.

The advantages of corms are that flowers are true to colour, need not be planted until September and are easier to grow in the earlier stages. Their disadvantages are, high cost of corms, and late flowering. At one time 'sleeping' corms were a great disadvantage but the new technique of storing at fairly high temperatures will prevent this trouble. Corms can still be very slow in starting into growth and in some cases it may be two months or more before all the corms have thrust the first leaf above the soil. To ensure good rooting, the soil temperature should be reasonably low—which is difficult in early September.

Production from seed can be sub-divided into:

    a) Direct sowing in permanent quarters.
    b) Sowing in pots or boxes and later planting in a glasshouse border or bed.

Before sowing the seed can be steeped in water heated to 70° F. for twenty-four hours or chitted in peat and sand (see 'Freesias from Seed').

Mobile Houses

Where mobile houses are available, they have proved very useful for freesia growing as the plants can grow in the open all summer and be covered with a heated house in the autumn. Transportable houses can also be used provided they can be heated to maintain a temperature of 50° F. in severe weather. Seed can be pre-chitted as described in 'Freesias from Seed'.

The area of the house should be marked out and divided into beds about 4 feet wide. These beds can be sown with pre-chitted seeds in May when the soil has become warm. Do not sow too early or the cold soil will retard germination and seeds may rot. Pre-chitting will help to get the seeds into growth very quickly and ensure a much better germination. If seeds cannot be chitted, they should be steeped for twenty-four hours in water heated to 70° F. This will help to soften the very hard seed coat and make it easier for the young root (*radicle*) to emerge through it. The soil should be covered with a thin layer (about ¼ in. to ½ in.) of moist peat to conserve moisture and prevent rapid drying out of the surface soil which would lead to erratic germination. Constant moisture content of the soil is a great help in assisting even germination.

During the summer, the seedlings must be kept free from weeds and the soil must not be allowed to get too dry. During hot weather, it may be necessary to use a spray line several times. When applying water, it should be remembered that a little water may do more harm than good by encouraging roots near the surface, therefore enough water to penetrate several inches of soil depth should be given. The equivalent of half an inch of rain (11,000 gallons per acre) should be applied over several hours, watering just before the plants really need it.

Pests must be watched for and, if found, the correct sprays must be given in good time to prevent damage. The plants must be given support as they develop and every care taken of them. In late September, the mobile house can be pulled over them.

Growing in mobile houses is a very good method for freesias, because it gives the advantages of ideal summer growth conditions with ideal winter conditions, for plants raised outdoors have a better constitution than those raised in glasshouses.

Seed can be sown pre-chitted or unchitted in the boxes, or pricked off from shallow seed trays as soon as convenient to handle.

The number of plants to allow per box should be approximately 18–20 per square foot of box area, though some growers do have a thicker plant than this. It is never wise to have plants too thick, for they will never develop properly under these conditions. Thick planting will mean smaller flower spikes and smaller flowers.

There is always a serious danger of the boxes drying out during hot weather and precautions must be taken to prevent this by watching the plants during hot dry spells. If there are a large number of boxes, it will be best to rig up an irrigation line which will do the job efficiently and with less likelihood of the boxes not being looked after. If the tips of the leaves show yellowing or browning, some damage has obviously occurred.

Large pots can be used in the same manner as boxes and they will need the same care as the boxes. It is important to stand the pots on a level foundation, or at least see that the rims of the pots are level, for only then will the plants receive enough water to get to the bottom of the pots. About an inch of space should be left between the top of the pot and the soil level.

The boxes or pots are taken into the heated houses or heated frames in September. Some growers remove the bottoms of the boxes so that the roots can ramify in the soil, after being brought into the greenhouses. Only a rich soil is suitable for this treatment.

Transplanting Systems

In these cases, plants are grown in pots and take the place of an early crop such as cucumbers or tomatoes when eth latter are finished. The difference between this method and the foregoing is that the plants and soil are tipped out from the pots into the soil in the beds or borders of the glasshouse where they will flower. It is better to transplant into the houses by the beginnng of August if possible so that the plants have plenty of time to develop before flowering begins. The plants do not get much of a check having been pot grown.

Seeds are sown as described earlier in this chapter allowing 4–5 seeds in a large 60 pot and about 6–7 seeds in a 48 or 5-in. pot. When transplanting, the plant density should be about the normal (170–180 per square yard of bed).

The advantage of this transplanting system is that plants can be brought along in smaller pots, thus occupying less space, and then take the place of an early crop such as cucumbers or early tomatoes.

Production from Corms

This is a very common method, but does not allow very many variations because corms must be planted in August or September, and they are nearly always planted *en situ* in beds in a heated glasshouse. Cool storage at 52° F. for 2–4 weeks after the usual warm-storage period will advance flowering by 10–12 days, but this is about the extent of the variation in flowering. If corms are planted late the foliage will be more soft and lush, due to lack of light, and it is better to plant at the normal time.

Pots can be used and a 6-in. (24) pot can be nearly filled with J.I.P. compost and 9–10 corms can be planted in each pot.

Little has been written about the best types of glass-houses for freesia cultivation, because few, if any, will wish to build special houses for what is, to most growers, a minor crop. As the freesia is mainly a winter-flowering subject, it should receive as much of the poor light available as possible. This means that the glasshouse should be light and airy with enough piping to give a minimum temperature of about 50° F. against an outside temperature of about 20° F., i.e. 12° of frost, or technically a 'lift' of 30° F. Growers may think this is much too low, but it is a minimum temperature when outdoor conditions are very severe.

Houses should be in good condition, thus avoiding losses of heat, and the entry of cold air should be restricted. Large panes of glass up to 2 ft. square will be of great assistance in maintaining the entry of the maximum amount of light. In smoky areas, the glass should be cleaned two or three times during the winter. Hydrofluoric acid at one part to twenty parts water is often used.

The thoughtful grower will use the system which best fits his own conditions, of labour, housing and marketing. If he is new to freesia growing, he will select one that appears to suit his needs and give it a small trial. At the end of the season, he may decide to try another system as the first one did not quite fulfil his needs. When he is certain he is on the right lines, he will increase the area of freesias each year until he gets to his pre-determined maximum.

Some growers will decide that freesia growing is not for them, and they will be right in most cases, for it is generally useless to grow a crop in which one has little interest or inclination. In a few years, it may be more difficult to make freesias pay, and only the keen grower will make a real success of it.

It may be useful to summarise the systems which are being used by growers at the present time:

a) Sowing direct in the soil and later covering with mobile glasshouses.
b) Sowing in large 7-8-in. pots or boxes and flowering the plants in these.
c) Sowing in 3-4-in. pots and planting out in August after a maiden crop.
d) Planting corms in glasshouses in September after tomatoes and cucumbers.
e) Planting corms in pots and flowering in these pots (not much used).

Most growers practice systems (b) and (d), but with the growing use of mobile houses, system (a) will probably be more widely used in the future. System (c) is a useful method and, though not widely practised, it is capable of giving very good results if care and attention are bestowed on it. It would be fatal, for instance, to delay planting out the freesias until say the end of September when natural growth is very slow indeed. Every month after June we get a slowing down of growth until September when light conditions alone present good growth. We can get a soft, spindly type of growth by forcing with artificial heat, but this type of growth is of little use to growers. Light and heat must always go hand in hand to produce sturdy and healthy growth. After the winter slowing down, we again find a resurgence of natural growth in glasshouses, beginning about the middle of January, and this growth becomes very rapid by April provided there is plenty of sunshine.

Systems based on plants from seed will give flowers from September onwards, and during recent years prices for freesias marketed in the autumn have been better than those produced in the late winter. The latter crops are mainly grown from corms. At the end of Chapter 2, growers will find a list of wholesale market prices based on weekly reports in the *Commercial Grower*, the well-known horticultural journal.

Some maintain that the best flowers are obtained from seedlings, while others support the reverse view—that the best flowers are cut from plants produced from corms. So much depends on how well the plants are grown. The good grower has an instinctive feel for his plants, and, by avoiding all excesses and also deficiencies, he gets the best out of them. Too much fussiness is not recommended, however, for then the grower becomes too conscious of their needs and cannot make up his mind as to when they need water, or feeding, or more heat, or ventilation. Moderation, or the 'golden mean' of the Greeks, is his best guide.

Plate 3. Growing from corms, general layout

Plate 4.   Method of supporting freesias

4. *Raising Freesias from Seed*

RAISING FREESIAS from seed is by far the cheaper method and is not so difficult, but it demands more care than raising plants from corms and growers quite often do not get a good 'stand' of plants. A seed is a tiny embryo plant contained in a seed coat and needs the correct environment to develop into a useful plant. Anyone who has had considerable experience in raising plants from seeds should not have any trouble in growing freesias from seed, but anyone who is not a good horticultural plantsman should take great care to eliminate all chances of failure as far as he can by following textbook methods.

The writer knows of cases which will illustrate how much depends on careful attention to details. Some growers have bought several pounds worth of seed, and, though they were very careful, they were only successful in germinating a few hundred seedlings. A small grower bought five shillings' worth of seed to try it out and succeeded in raising 96 plants! This was very good indeed but the explanation lay in the fact that the second grower had always been a craftsman and had raised many different kinds of plants for many years.

The usual time to sow freesia seeds is from March 15th to early June. The seeds sown early will produce plants which will flower from September onwards. Seeds sown later will flower from Christmas onwards.

The number of seeds in an ounce is approximately 2,600–2,800. A good mixture usually consists of 40 per cent yellow, 30 per cent blue and 30 per cent red. Yellow is a dominant colour and brightens up a bunch of freesias, while red and blue flowers necessary to give variety do not have much impact on the buyer. The seeds of yellow varieties are fewer per ounce and average only about 2,500 per ounce, while red and blue varieties have many more seeds per ounce. Seeds can be bought in separate colours or in mixture. Amateurs can buy 100 seeds for 5/-. Nurserymen usually purchase by the ounce (28·35 grms.) A kilogram of seed will contain 100,000 seeds.

Before going into the propagation composts which may be used, it is worth while considering the factors of successful germination. Three things are essential for the successful germination of a seed—air, warmth and moisture. No seed can develop without these conditions. Air is necessary because seeds breathe just as animals do, taking in oxygen and giving out carbon dioxide, in other words they respire. Warmth is necessary and every kind of seed has its optimum germination temperature. Weed seeds will grow at temperatures of 40 to 45° F., but plants such as cucumbers require about 70° F. to develop properly. The optimum temperature for freesia germination is about 68 to 70° F., though they will grow at lower and higher temperatures. The third condition for successful germination is moisture, for no seed will grow if it is kept dry and many seeds absorb their own bulk in water before they are ready to 'sprout'. Trials in Denmark showed that at 54° F. only 20 per cent of the seeds germinated and at 86° F. again only 20 per cent germinated. The best temperature was 68° F. (20° C.).

Seeds generally germinate best in the dark and this is true of the freesia. The boxes of seeds are usually covered over with a sheet of glass and brown paper on top.

A compost for freesia seeds should be light and well aerated and in practice this means a compost such as the John Innes compost. The John Innes seed compost is two parts loam, one part peat and one part sand with 1½ oz. of superphosphate and ¾ oz. ground chalk per bushel of compost. Generally a suitable compost would consist of a medium loam with peat and sand added to give moisture-holding and good aeration qualities. This is true of the John Innes composts.

There are two methods of raising freesias from seeds, one is by sowing directly into the compost and the other is by chitting the seeds in moist peat and then picking out the chitted seeds and sowing them into boxes, pots, or in beds in a glasshouse.

Growers may sow direct into 3-in. pots (60s) for planting in beds in September, in 5-in. pots (48s) and in deep boxes in which the plants will flower. Large pots 7 in. to 9 in. are also used and these are moved into the glasshouse at the end of the summer.

3-in. or 60 pots	3–5 seeds per pot
5-in or 48	5–7
7-in. to 8-in.	9–12
Boxes at least	
6 in. deep	20 seeds per square foot

When sown unchitted all seeds will probably not germinate so it will be necessary to allow extra seeds. When germination is complete remove weakest seedlings and any albinos which arise. When using chitted seed, there should be 100 per cent stand of plants so that the exact number may be sown per pot or box.

After sowing, cover compost with about half an inch of moist peat to prevent rapid drying out of the compost. Freesia seed usually takes some weeks before all seeds have germinated and it is better to avoid watering any more than one can help before the seedlings appear above the soil. Do not be dismayed if a few shoots appear after a couple of weeks. If the environment is correct (air, temperature and humidity) more will appear later. If the weather is bright, cover the boxes with sacking or other material to keep the seeds in darkness.

It is certainly safer to chit seed before sowing in receptacles and this can be done as follows: Moisten some horticultural peat and after soaking the seeds in water heated to a temperature of 70° F. mix them with the peat and keep them in a temperature of 70° F. in a glasshouse. When many seeds have chitted, remove them and sow them in pots, boxes or beds. Chitting has taken place when the radicle or young root of the embryo plant has emerged from the seed. The chitted seed can be sown in pots, boxes, in beds in greenhouses, or in the open ground later in the season.

Another method which is used on the Continent is to use boxes a few inches deep and cover the bottoms with moist peat. Then damp filter paper is spread on the peat and seeds are sown on the filter paper and left until they are chitted. The box is covered with glass to prevent rapid evaporation and the glass covered by cardboard to keep out light. Where many boxes are used they may be stacked on top of each other.

The compost in which freesias will be permanently planted and in which they will flower should be richer than that recommended for sowing seeds. A John Innes potting compost may be used and the formula of this is as follows:

> 7 parts good turfy loam (steamed).
> 3 parts horticultural peat.
> 2 parts sharp sand (coarse), plus John Innes Base Fertilizer at 5 lb. per cubic yard of compost, and 1 lb. chalk per cubic yard.

This is John Innes Potting Compost 1 (JI P1). If double the amount of J.I. base fertiliser is given the compost becomes No. 2 or J.I. P2. Many growers have their own

Plate 5. Picking the blooms

Plate 6. Grown from seed

special composts but most of them are variations of the John Innes composts. A few have old rotted farmyard manure in them with consequently less fertiliser.

Although John Innes composts are standardised composts, the limiting factor is the loam itself which varies from district to district—even in the same field or garden. The best loam is the top 4–6 ins. of top soil from a meadow which has been under grass for twenty to fifty years. This should be stacked in a heap for about six months before use. It may be very acid or lacking in phosphates or potash. A sample can be checked by the National Agricultural Advisory Service in the case of commercial growers and by the County Farm Institute in respect of private gardeners. It is essential to know if it is acid as freesias prefer the compost to be about pH 6·5 which can be termed very slightly acid—pH 7·0 being neutral and all values above 7·0 show alkalinity.   It is recommended that loam for John Innes composts should be brought to a pH of 6·3 before making into a compost. If the loam is acid when stacked, each layer of loam should be dusted with lime as the stack is built. The amount of lime required will be given by the advisory officer concerned.

Generally, any deficiency of phosphates or potash are taken care of by the John Innes base fertiliser, but if the loam is very deficient extra phosphates or potash may have to be added. Phosphates are very necessary to young seedlings as they stimulate root action and general development. Potash hardens a soft plant and makes it more resistant to disease attack.

Some sow freesia seeds fairly thickly in seed trays and prick-off the small seedlings some weeks later into their permanent quarters, i.e. large pots, boxes or beds.

It may be useful to summarise the usual methods of raising freesias from seeds.

Pre-chitting Seeds

a) Mixing seeds with moist peat and placing in a temperature of 68–78° F.
b) Sowing seeds on filter paper placed on moist peat in in a temperature of 68–78° F.

Unchitted Seeds

a) Soaking seeds for twenty-four hours in water warmed to 70° F., then sowing.
b) Sowing fairly thickly in seed boxes and pricking-off later.

All the above methods are used by different growers but one of the pre-chitting methods is usually more certain to get a good stand of plants.

When sowing chitted seeds in beds they may be sown in rows lengthwise along the bed or in rows crosswise. Sow in rows about half an inch deep and allow 1½ in. between each seed or roughly 25 per yard run of row. The rows of seeds are usually 4–5 ins. apart. This will make a planting density of about 170–180 seeds per square yard which is useful as a guide to the number of seeds required. After sowing, cover with a layer of peat about half an inch thick. This will help to prevent rapid drying-out if the weather is dry and sunny. Seeds never germinate well if there are rapid changes of moisture and dryness in the soil or compost. The pre-chitting of the seeds means a much more even germination but, even so, all the young shoots will not come up at the same time.

When seeds are sown unchitted and fairly thickly in boxes, for pricking-off later into pots or boxes, care should be taken to see that they are kept under good germinating conditions and that pricking-off is carried out as soon as the seedlings are able to be handled easily. If they are allowed to become too large there will be considerable damage to their root systems when they are being lifted for transplanting. In any case, freesias do not take too kindly to transplanting and it is usually better to pre-chit and avoid moving the plants. The freesia, like all members of the monocotyledon division of plants, first shows above the soil as a single small green leaf. Later this develops and another leaf originates from the base of the first one.

It is usual to remove the peat which was used to cover the seed bed after about twelve days so that the young leaves can get the sun and air when they emerge from the soil.

Once the seedlings are well through the soil there should be little fear of anything going wrong. Freesia seedlings are actually quite sturdy, and, provided they are not allowed to suffer from either too much or too little water, there should be no real worries.

5. *Raising Freesias from Corms*

IT IS MORE expensive to grow freesias from corms in the first year but as the corms can be ripened off and grown for several years afterwards, their cost should be spread over three to five years or more. Some growers sell off some of their corms and keep the remainder for flower production. Their size is usually 4½ to 6 cms.

The main advantage when growing from corms is that they need not be planted until September. This means that no labour is required during the busy spring months and the grower can wait until he has cleared an early crop of, for instance, cucumbers or tomatoes. For a beginner, growing from corms will probably be easier than growing from seed.

Until recently a trouble known as 'sleepiness' made growing from corms more hazardous than it is today. Corms suffering from 'sleepiness' remain in the soil in a dormant condition and do not form any roots or shoots. Daffodil growers have seen similar symptoms after bulbs have been over 'sterilised' during the hot-water treatment. It appears from research work carried out in Holland that the growing point thickens as the food reserve moves towards it and forms a new corm over the old one. During this period which may last from six to ten months no flowering shoots are produced.

Dutch research workers have found that the trouble can be overcome by warm storage after lifting. A temperature of 78° F. for a minimum period of ten weeks will overcome the trouble. The atmospheric moisture should not go below 60 per cent and this can best be done by having water in containers in the store which can be used to moisten sacking in the storeroom. The corms are placed in boxes during the treatment and to ensure even heat treatment the boxes should be re-stacked two or three times during the ten-weeks' storage period.

Considerable research has been carried out on inducing early flowering of freesia corms both in Europe and Japan. It has been found that if the storage temperature is increased to 86° F. and the corms kept at this figure for fourteen to fifteen weeks, the flowering time will be advanced. The yield and size of the flowers will also be improved.

More drastic treatment will put forward the flowering date by twelve days or more but will have a bad effect on flower quantity and quality and is not recommended. If a grower wants flowers early in the season he should grow from seed. This drastic treatment consists of giving the corms cold-storage (after the warm-storage) treatment of 52° F. for two to four days before planting.

Different varieties behave in different ways after cold treatment and some varieties, if cool-treated and planted in July or August, will produce flowers in December. Soil temperature is very important, and if on the warm side rooting will be delayed with consequent later flowering. All bulbs root better when soil temperatures are low.

Pupation

If freesia corms are kept at low temperature, a young bulblet is formed on the old corm.

This phenomenon is called 'pupation' by the Dutch and not only happens in the soil but also when corms are kept in boxes in the warehouse. If desired, the grower can use this process for propagating purposes.

If corms, which are lifted in the spring after forcing, are stored from June onwards at a temperature of 52–60° F., complete bulblets will form by January or February. In order to ensure an even growth, these bulblets should be stored for twelve to thirteen weeks at 75° F. and then planted at the end of May in the open. By covering the beds with glass in September, it is possible to have flowers fit to cut in October. During the warm treatment it is necessary to see that the relative moisture does not drop below 55° F.

Only undamaged corms should be used on all these treatments.

Covering the soil after planting with a layer of straw will help to keep down the soil temperature but must be removed when the young shoots are not more than one inch high or they will be damaged during the removal of the straw.

Corms are purchased by size and the usual commercial sizes are 6 c.m.

The corms are planted in August and September in beds about 4 ft. wide. They may be planted lengthwise or across the beds but planting crosswise takes longer as there are a large number of short rows. Drills 2 in. deep are made and the corms are pressed into the bottom of the drill. It is usual to make the drills 3–4 in. apart and to allow about 2 in. between the corms. If the weather is sunny it may be necessary to cover the beds with a thin layer of moist peat to prevent rapid evaporation. Keep the house temperature down to about 60° F. as far as conditions will permit.

The corms will start showing growth above the soil about two weeks after planting but there will still be many blank spaces to fill. It will probably be six to eight weeks or longer before all the corms have pushed their green shoots above the soil so new growers should not get too worried. The temperature should be kept around 50–55° F. once the shoots appear to prevent rapid and soft growth which would spoil the crop.

With the very large so-called 'super freesias', some growers plant 4 in. square to allow more space for development. These 'super freesias' are of Dutch origin and the stems reach a height of 3 feet.

Freesias are unable to support their own weight and as soon as growth is about 4 in high, a system of supporting wires must be given. Some growers use thin galvanised wire run lengthwise along the bed and then have rayon string across the wires to form small squares. The ends of the wires can be attached to a piece of wood the same length as the bed is wide. This stick can be fastened temporarily to posts at each end of the bed and raised as the plants grow taller.

Some growers prefer to plant in the Dutch bed system, that is, by removing the soil to a depth of $1\frac{1}{2}$ ins. to $1\frac{3}{4}$in. and placing the corms in the new bed surface at the usual distances. The next bed is then prepared, only this time the soil is placed over the corms in the first planted bed. It will now be a little higher than it was originally because of the corms and the loosened soil but it will settle down and consolidate itself in due course.

When the plants are in flower, it is a good time to rogue or cull out the off-types, wrong varieties or colours, and also any plants affected with virus disease. The corms will probably be used on the same nursery for several years. After that, some growers prefer to get a new stock either by buying new corms or by raising plants from seed.

After flowering has finished, the plants should be left some seven or eight weeks before they are lifted and stored. It should be remembered that when flowering has finished the new corms are still small and require the further seven or eight weeks to complete their growth. Watering must be reduced but only gradually to encourage the ripening of the corms or bulbs. When ready to lift the foliage is removed and then the corms are dug-up. After lifting, the corms should not be left in the sun or it will affect their performance in the following season. They should be placed in a shed, then cleaned and sorted out preparatory to being stored in a warm temperature.

6. *General Management*

THE PROBLEMS of general management of freesias usually begin in September when plants raised from seeds are brought into the greenhouses, and corms are producing shoots, also in greenhouses. Glasshouses, having an artificial climate, can spoil normal growth unless steps are taken to control their climate. Too much heat or humidity will cause soft growth which is useless for producing firm flowering shoots.

A temperature around 50–55° F. will be quite warm enough and will encourage sturdy growth. The weather has an effect on the glasshouse and in bright sunshine the temperature will rise by 5–10° F. even with ventilation, and because of the high light conditions these higher temperatures will not do any harm, in fact, they may do considerable good. On the other hand, if the weather is cold and sunless, it will be better to drop the temperature by 5–10° F., to 45–50° F.

In glasshouses it is always a safe rule to balance light and heat. Heat without strong light will produce spindly growth which must not be tolerated. Artificial illumination, though used for tomato and cucumber seedlings is not usual for freesias as it is not necessary. But if such illumination was used the temperature could be raised considerably. It is likely that artificial light will be used for many plants in the dark weather in the future. The development of cheaper types of lamps, without the need for expensive chokes for each lamp, will encourage growers to use them more widely.

Freesias can tolerate lower temperatures than most flower crops under glass, and, on occasions an odd degree of frost has not done any serious harm to the crop.

Plate 7. Preparing for packing in Cornwall

Plate 8. Packing for market in Cornwall

It is usual to avoid giving the plants much water until the flower-buds are noticed. This does not mean that they must be kept fairly dry as this would be harmful, only that watering should be curtailed as far as possible. When watering, care must be taken to avoid splashing the flowers or foliage, or the ever-present spores of Botrytis will attack weak spots in the plants and cause serious losses.

The plants must be well supported or the stems will become twisted and broken. There are several ways of doing this and these include:

a) Square net system as used for carnations.
b) Netting stretched over posts.
c) Brushwood or canes in pots.

With the carnation system the 'net' can be stationary or capable of being moved upwards as the plants grow taller. A simple plan for stationary supports is to drive in stakes around the bed and stretch strong galvanised wire between the stakes about 6–12 in. from the soil level. Then rayon or cotton twine (carnation type) is stretched in both directions lengthwise along the bed and also across the bed. Two or more 'nets' may be necessary.

When the supports are to be moved up with the growth, the wires and cord are attached at each end of the bed to a crosspiece of wood. This crosspiece can be raised and fastened to uprights at the ends of the bed.

Some growers stretch wire-netting or cord over the beds and fasten it to posts around the bed.

The marketing of freesias may extend from late August until the beginning of May, beginning with early-sown plants and ending with September-planted corms. Marketing does not present any serious difficulty because they are not difficult flowers to pack. It is important to cut the flower stems at the right time. If they are cut too early the youngest buds at the end of the spike may not open because they are not well enough developed when their food supply is cut off. It is usual to cut the spikes when two or three of the earliest flowers are fairly open.

The colour composition of the bunch of 12–15 spikes is very important because the appeal and scent of the bunch is mainly a matter of colour. The yellow and orange varieties possess the greatest amount of scent and they are also the most dominant colours. Blues and reds are smaller and are not so showy, and also have much less scent. This means that each market bunch must be balanced to appear attractive to the buyer. Some growers have beds of separate colours, and when freesias are grown on a fairly large scale this is a useful method of ensuring a balanced supply of the various colours to make the most attractive bunches. Bunches without the rich scented yellow and orange flowers would look very dull and give off little perfume!

Many growers have found that freesias travel best if packed in a dry state, and that any loss of turgidity resulting soon disappears when they are placed in water by the florist. No foliage is included with the flower spikes. The bunches are packed in boxes lined with grease-proof paper and soft tissue paper is used to pack the bunches.

7. Pests and Diseases and Other Troubles

THERE ARE a number of pests and diseases and also some cultural troubles which affect freesias and must be dealt with. The best way to deal with pests is to take action as soon as a few are seen, and not to wait until they have increased to considerable proportions. Any plant growing under artificial conditions is very likely to be a prey to pests, and a constant watch should be kept.

Diseases are more deep seated as a rule, and precautions and preventive measures are the best means of defence. When purchasing bulbs, the grower should see that they are really sound, and if the sample examined contains diseased specimens, no purchase should be made.

Some troubles arise from cultural defects such as too much fertiliser, or keeping the soil too wet or too dry. Too high a nitrogen content will also cause poor stems and soft foliage.

Aphids is one pest which is found at one time or another in all glasshouses and species of both Myzus and Macrosiphon may be found on freesias. These aphids, or green fly, or plant lice, as they are variously called, suck the sap from the plants, as they have mouth parts which are specially constructed for sucking sap. They multiply exceedingly quickly and should never be neglected.

Control may be by sprays, smokes, or aerosols, and the substances used include nicotine, B.H.C. (Benzene hexachloride), parathion and others.

Thrips (T. *tobaci*) can do considerable damage to freesias by attacking the foliage, and may attack the flowers

causing small white flecks. Control of thrips is usually by
D.D.T., or parathion* smokes.

During recent years virus diseases have become much
more widespread, and are now quite a serious problem in
freesias. There are apparently two distinct viruses, Phaseolus virus 2 and Freesia virus. The first named is not so well
known but does considerable damage. Mr. Van Koot has
written an account of freesia virus and states that the
majority of cultivated varieties show a leaf mosaic with
Phaseolus virus 2. Some varieties such as Bronze Giant
show apparent virus symptoms, but virus is not confirmed
when serological tests are made. He also says that freesia
virus was transmitted by the aphid Macrosiphon eurphor-
biae.

The best methods of controlling virus are by:

a) Selection of healthy corms.
b) Destroying infected plants during the flowering
period or just afterwards.
c) Control of aphis by spraying or by smokes.

Virus can cause 'breaking' of the flowers in the same
way that virus in tulip shows. In tulips, it was demon-
strated that there could be colour adding, or colour removal by virus. In white or yellow flowers, red stripes would
develop, and in red flowers, white or yellow stripes appear.
In freesias, the affected flowers show a striped effect
because the colours are 'broken' by the virus.

What is believed to be another symptom of virus disease
shows as water-soaked spots on the leaves, which later
dry up and become white and papery. In severe cases, the
spots coalesce and the foliage is killed, and any blooms
which manage to open are distorted. This disease was

* If parathion sprays or aerosols are used, suitable precautions must
be taken, these include the use of protective clothing such as gloves,
gas-masks, rubber boots, etc.

Plate 9.   Another form of packing, corrugated
fibreboard

Plate 10.   Prize winner in Guernsey, best exhibit
in show, 1954

written up by H. G. Langford in 1927, and mentioned by Kenneth Smith in *A Textbook of Virus Diseases* published in 1937. Though some say it is not a disease, it is admitted that a diseased stock gives rise to affected plants and that seedlings are free in the first year. As a rule, virus is not carried in the seed, though it can be carried *on* the seed, that is, on the seed coat. Another scientist, Dr. R. C. Woodward interested himself in this trouble and thought it was a virus disease of which the vector was *Myzus convolvuli Kalt.*, an aphid.

A species of Fusarium is not uncommon, and causes a corm rot which brings about wilting and finally the death of the plant. Affected corms show spots which penetrate to the centre of the corm. This trouble was described as far back as 1933 by writers in the U.S.A. Corms should be bought from a reputable dealer and inspected on arrival.

Another disease which affects freesias is Botrytis, which is always with us. Good ventilation and scrupulous cleanliness is the best method of avoiding the trouble. Septoria gladioli, or hard rot, is occasionally found in freesias, as also is Penicillium gladioli which is usually a storage trouble.

Non-parasitic Troubles

These troubles can be termed cultural and they are a common source of difficulty to many growers, especially those of limited experience. Both the plant pathologist and the entomologist often say that these troubles are not their concern. They are not, of course, but a grower wants to know how to get rid of them and he does not care who suggests the remedial measures.

One serious trouble which affects freesias is that known as pC or soluble salts in excess. When a soil is given annual applications of fertilisers containing large quantities of sulphates without plenty of winter flooding, the amount of

D

soluble salts in the soil becomes too high for normal plant growth. In extreme cases, very high concentrations of soluble salts can cause the death of the plant. If there is any excess of chloride in the soil, the effect of these soluble salts can be greatly increased with disastrous results on the crop. Freesias are very sensitive to excess soluble salts.

The measurement of soluble salts is made on a scale known as the pC scale. Other examples of this type of scale is the pH or acidity scale and the pF or water measurement in soil scale. They are all logarithmic scales so that a pC of 2·60 represents ten times as great a concentration of salt as a pC of 3.60.

This means that the difference of a few units can make a very great difference. Field soils are generally about 3·50 or lower, but many old glasshouse soils are getting down to pC 2·70 which is near the danger line.

These soluble salt troubles can be avoided by using soil from outdoors or by thoroughly flooding any glasshouse soils before use. The N.A.A.S. will arrange for the pC values to be determined so that a grower can always know where he stands.

Excessive nitrogen in the compost can cause local thickening of freesia flower stems and eventually splitting of the stem itself. Do not add too much nitrogen to the soil. Most growers use John Innes potting compost No. 2. Extra nitrogen, if needed, can be added later.

The soil should never be too acid and a pH of 6.3-7·0 will be quite suitable. The John Innes composts generally work out about pH 6·3, depending on the loam used. A pH of 7·0 is neutral and all values below 7·0 are acid, and those above 7·0 are alkaline. A pH of 6·0 has ten units of acidity and pH of 5·0 has 100 and a pH of 4.0 1,000 units of acidity. This is by reason of our logarithmic scale again! Many peats show an acid reaction of 3·5 while others are less acid. English or German peats give very good results.

Temperatures are very important and during the dark winter days 45–50° F. are ample and should not be exceeded. If there is sunlight, a rise of 5–10° F. will not do any harm. Slow and sturdy growth can only be secured by keeping the temperature low. Quick and soft growth is fatal to quality flowers on good stems, and such conditions also encourage attacks of pests and diseases. In very severe weather the temperature can go down to nearly freezing without any serious results.

8. *Freesia Growing for Amateurs*

AMATEURS with a cool greenhouse can grow freesias quite easily especially from corms. Those with more experience can also raise plants from seed which is cheaper and more interesting. One enthusiastic amateur known to the writer bought 100 seeds and obtained over 90 plants which is very good indeed. A novice would not expect to get a germination percentage as high as this.

Freesias can be grown in the garden during the summer months if specially treated bulbs are used, but many will not want freesias in the summer when there are so many other flowers available.

Probably pot-grown plants are best as they can be taken into the home without having to cut the flowers. The medium 48 or 5-in. pot is a useful size, as it is not too large to carry about or to find vases or bowls to fit around it. The corms are purchased in August or early September as soon as they are available and always buy from a good firm, for there are large numbers of inferior bulbs of all kinds on the market and advertised in the popular Press. These bulbs are cheap but many will be too small to flower and others may be infected with disease. It is a waste of time to grow such bulbs, for they require as much heat and attention as good ones, and give a very poor return for the efforts spent in trying to grow them.

Five corms can be planted in each 5-in. pot. The pots can be filled with John Innes potting compost No. 2, or more simply J.I.P.2. The number two compost means that double the amount of John Innes base fertiliser is mixed into the compost. The compost is as follows:

7 parts loam (or top spit soil cut from old pasture
and stacked for six months and steamed.

3 parts horticultural peat.

2 parts coarse sand.

plus $\frac{3}{4}$ oz. ground chalk; $1\frac{1}{2}$ oz. superphosphate
(16% P205); $1\frac{1}{2}$ oz. hoof and horn ($\frac{1}{8}$-in. grist);
$\frac{3}{4}$ oz. sulphate of potash.

per bushel of compost. (For J.I.P.1.)

The 5-in. pots are recommended for bringing into the
home but, of course, 6-in., 7-in. or 8-in. pots can be used
and will accommodate more corms. For instance, an 8-in.
pot can hold 9–10 corms.

Rooting of all bulbs is encouraged by cool conditions
and the pots should be kept in a temperature not exceed-
ing 60° F. This may be difficult if the weather is still
warm, but the pots need not be kept in a glasshouse.

The young shoots will begin to appear in two to three
weeks and the pots can then be kept in a cool frame if
there is no fear of frost, but if frost does threaten, the
pots must be taken into the house and placed in a window
which faces south or south-west. All plants hate draughts
and this is sometimes a problem but can be overcome.
Gas is worse, and so the kitchen is out if there is a gas-
stove there. The plants will require a few pieces of brushwood to support them as they develop. The twigs can be
contained by a piece of green string around the outside
of the twigs and plants.

Watering is always a problem to amateurs as nearly
everyone asks 'How often should I water my freesias?'
This is an impossible question to answer because so much
depends on the temperature, the humidity, and the growth
of the plants themselves. But it is useless to give plants
water every two days or every week. They must only be
given water when they need it. This can be found by

tapping the pots sharply with the knuckles or with a small piece of wood on a cane. When a plant is dry, the pot gives a hollow sound, but if it is moist there is no response, only a dead type of noise.

Freesias should not be given much water while the buds are being formed, but as soon as the flower spikes appear they must have more water. A temperature of 45–50° F. should be about correct. A fall of 5° F. at night will not do any harm. If the plants are in a window, the curtains should be pulled during severe weather or the plants can be moved away from the window. If fortunate enough to possess a heated greenhouse, the amateur grower should not have much trouble in producing freesias if a temperature of 45° F. can be held in cold frosty weather. If worried about very severe weather, it will be helpful to place thin plastic sheeting on the north and east sides of the glasshouse, or cover the glass with hessian or canvas. Many greenhouses are heated with oil-type stoves and those with a water container are best as this prevents the house becoming too 'dry'. A certain amount of humidity is necessary for good plant growth.

Amateurs can also raise freesias from seed and 100 seeds of the finest strains can be bought for 5/–.

Seeds can be sown in pots in April or May and the resultant plants will begin to flower in October or November. The advantage here is that the plants will develop during the summer months when growth conditions are ideal, and, when they are taken into the greenhouse in late September they are almost nearly to flower.

Freesia seeds are very hard and it is helpful to good germination to steep the seeds in water heated to 70° F. for twenty-four hours before sowing. A 5-in pot with John Innes compost can be allowed 5–7 seeds spaced 1½ in. apart. Later, if all do germinate, the plants can be reduced to five! After sowing, keep the pots in a temperature of as near 68° F. (20° C.) as possible, until the young shoots show above the soil—which may take two to three weeks.

Another method is to mix up a little moist peat and sand and work in the freesia seeds in this mixture. A pot or other container will do well enough to hold the mixture of peat, sand, and seeds. Keep the whole in a temperature of 68° F. Examine the seeds periodically and remove the sprouted seeds and sow in pots as before.

The plants raised from seeds can be treated as advised for the plants grown from corms from the time they are brought into the greenhouse or home.

For providing cut flowers, freesias may be grown in boxes 6–7 in. deep, and filling the boxes with J.I.P.2 compost as described earlier in this chapter. The number of plants allowed to a box depends on the size of the box, but if 20 per square foot are allowed for final flowering everything will be all right. If one is growing in separate colours, allow more when sowing blue or red freesias as these are weaker growing than the yellow and orange shades. The yellow varieties have the strongest scent. Most amateurs, however, will be growing mixed strains, but when larger quantities are grown separate colours may be preferred. A bright bunch of freesias should have a fair proportion of yellow and orange shades because these colours are dominant and assertive. A bunch of blues and reds in various hues would look rather dull beside a bunch containing a few in the yellow spectrum. Flowers of red and blue shades are also smaller.

The boxes could be left outdoors during the summer and apart from watering when necessary, and weeding, would not require any attention. In late September the boxes would be brought into the glasshouse. They would not need any artificial heat until some weeks had passed— depending on the weather, of course. Freesias do not require much heat, and a temperature of 45–50° F. would be quite enough. This temperature could rise to 60° F. or more in bright sunshine, even with the ventilators open.

Generally, it does not take much heat to maintain 45–50° F. except in very severe weather. This usually occurs in January and February, for, until Christmas, our climate is fairly mild, particularly south of the Wash and also along the west coast. Freesias would only be part of the crop in the greenhouse as there would be overwintering plants and probably bulbs in pots and bowls, also bedding plants for a summer display. The winter is the time when we appreciate flowers most, and the small expense would be worth while.

Amateurs can grow freesias outdoors during the summer months if they purchase bulbs specially prepared for this purpose. These are available from most seedsmen in the spring at 7/6 per dozen, and are planted in April or May.

The cost of freesia corms for planting in the autumn is 5/- to 6/- per dozen or 35/- to 45/- per 100. Many firms will supply half a dozen corms at the dozen rate and 50 at the 100 rate.

The following freesias are available in small quantities: pink and red hybrids, blue and mauve hybrids, white and cream hybrids, and a rainbow mixture of all colours. There are also named varieties including the well-known Buttercup. Many named varieties will be on sale shortly.

Index

Acidity, see pH   *page* 46

Amateurs:
  growing in Glasshouses for   48
  growing in summer, outdoors   52

Boxes:
  for freesia growing   51
  depth required   51

Composts:
  John Innes seed   30
  John Innes potting   32

Chemicals for Pest Control:
  B.H.C.   43
  D.D.T.   44
  parathion   43-4

Corms:
  cost of, for amateurs   52
  planting   38
  pupation   37
  'sleepiness   36

Diseases:
  Botrytis   45
  Fusarium   45
  Hard Rot   45
  Penicillium   45
  Virus   44

Dutch Bed system   39

Freesia Breeding   14
  Capital outlay   19
  Cut flowers, as   15

Freesia Breeding—*continued*
Glasshouses for   *page* 26
Labour needs   17–18
refracta   11–14
strains   12
Varieties   12

Fertilizers, too much   43

Flowers:
colour composition of bunches   42
'breaking' by virus   44

Germination conditions   30
temperatures   30

History   11

Kilogram of seeds   30

Nitrogen   46

Packing   42

Pests:
Aphis   43
Thrips   43

Physiological troubles:
pH   46
pC or soluble salts   45

Plants per square yard of bed   34

Pre-chitting seeds   32
on filter paper   32

Production from corms   25

Roguing plants   39

Seeds per pot when sowing   31
per ounce   29

Sowing   29

Sowing in pots   31

Strains of freesias	*page* 12
Storage temperatures of corms	36–7
Supporting plants	39
Super freesias	38
Temperatures:	
storage	36–7
cultural	47–52
Transplanting systems	25–7
Virus	44
Watering	49–50

ISBN 978-1-44374-100-2

9 781443 741002

A Selection of Old-Time Recipes for Toffee Sweets

Various